P9-DMA-053

SUGAR AND MICE AND THINGS-NOT-SO-NICE ARE WHAT SOME LITTLE KIDS DIG

Dear Folks and Grandma:

Today is Tuesday. Evelyn threw up at breakfast and Rhoda had to go to the infirmary with a bloody nose after the pool because Shirley tried to hold her head down and Denise spilled a bottle of ketchup on Sandra during lunch.

We had a flood in the bathroom and Harriet tied Louise's shoes together.

More tomorrow about Wednesday.

Love,
Mary

DIRTY HANDS AND DIRTY FACES...KIDS LEAVE THEIR MARK IN THE ODDEST PLACES.

JUST TURN THE PAGE
IT'S ALL THE RAGE.
YOU'LL FIND OUR KIDS
ARE PRETTY SAGE.

More Humor from SIGNET

☐ **STILL MORE LETTERS FROM CAMP.** Bestselling collector of humor, Bill Adler, and cartoonist, Syd Hoff, once again join forces to bring you this hilarious new gathering of gems from the kids at camp. (#T5651—75¢)

☐ **HIP KIDS' LETTTERS FROM CAMP by Bill Adler.** It's a groove, it's a wild trip, it's Bill Adler's newest and nuttiest mailbag collection from those far-out campers. (#T5483—75¢)

☐ **RIGHT ON! WEE PALS #3.** The first integrated comic strip to be syndicated in American newspapers. WEE PALS presents a child's-eye view of the contemporary scene with humor, vast insight and a good dose of philosophy. (#T5305—75¢)

☐ **OVER SEXTEEN #4 edited by J. M. Elgart.** The fourth hilarious OVER SEXTEEN, and the funniest yet, comprised of jokes and cartoons for people who are over "sexteen." (#Q4458—95¢)

☐ **CHARLIE BROWN'S ALL STARS by Charles M. Schulz.** Linus, Lucy, Frieda, Shermy, Snoopy and Charlie Brown himself—the whole team that delights millions of fans in the popular cartoon strip are on deck in this story of an all-star baseball team and its conscientious but misunderstood manager. In full color. (#T4256—75¢)

THE NEW AMERICAN LIBRARY, INC.,
P.O. Box 999, Bergenfield, New Jersey 07621

Please send me the SIGNET BOOKS I have checked above. I am enclosing $_____(check or money order—no currency or C.O.D.'s). Please include the list price plus 25¢ a copy to cover handling and mailing costs. (Prices and numbers are subject to change without notice.)

Name_____

Address_____

City_____State_____Zip Code_____
Allow at least 3 weeks for delivery

MORE LETTERS FROM CAMP

Edited by *BILL ADLER*

Illustrated by *SYD HOFF*

A SIGNET BOOK from
NEW AMERICAN LIBRARY
TIMES MIRROR

Illustrations copyright © 1966 by The New American Library, Inc.

Copyright © Bill Adler, 1966

All rights reserved. No part of this book may be reproduced without written permission from the publishers.

Library of Congress Catalog Card Number: 66-25112

This is a reprint of a hardcover edition published by The New American Library, Inc.

 SIGNET TRADEMARK REG. U.S. PAT. OFF. AND FOREIGN COUNTRIES
REGISTERED TRADEMARK—MARCA REGISTRADA
HECHO EN CHICAGO, U.S.A.

SIGNET, SIGNET CLASSICS, SIGNETTE, MENTOR AND PLUME BOOKS are published by The New American Library, Inc., 1301 Avenue of the Americas, New York, New York 10019

FIRST PRINTING, JUNE, 1967

9 10 11 12 13 14 15 16

PRINTED IN THE UNITED STATES OF AMERICA

Ever since the publication of
<u>Letters from Camp</u> I have been deluged
with thousands of letters from parents
around the country asking me to put
together a second volume of camp
letters and to please include their
youngster's letter.

So to keep faith with those parents
and their friends, we have selected
the funniest letters we have received
in the last four years for this book
of all new--all hilarious--all genuine
letters written by hearty, active
uninhibited summer campers from Maine
to California.

Bill Adler
New York City
April, 1966

To my son Billy, Jr., and his

stalwart fellow bunkmates

at Camp Wildwood

DEAR FOLKS,

   I AM FINE. THERE
HASN'T BEEN A SICK KID IN
  THE BUNK ALL DAY

    LOVE,
     MELISSA

DEAR FOLKS AND GRANDMA,

  TODAY IS TUESDAY. EVELYN THREW
UP AT BREAKFAST AND RHODA HAD
TO GO TO THE INFIRMARY WITH A
 BLOODY NOSE AFTER BREAKFAST.
MELISSA ALMOST DROWNED IN THE
POOL BECAUSE SHIRLEY TRIED TO
HOLD HER HEAD DOWN AND DENISE
 SPILLED A BOTTLE OF KETCHUP ON
SANDRA DURING LUNCH.

  WE HAD A FLOOD IN THE BATHROOM
AND HARRIET TIED LOUISE'S SHOES
     TOGETHER.

 MORE TOMORROW ABOUT WEDNESDAY

   LOVE,
    MARY

Dear Dad,

We went on an overnight hike in the woods and I wasn't afraid of sleeping in the woods. I stayed up all night.

Richie

HELLO FATHER,

MONDAY WE WENT ON AN ALL-DAY HIKE. TUESDAY WE HAD RUNNING RACES. WEDNESDAY WE PLAYED FOOTBALL AND BASEBALL. THURSDAY WE HAD ANOTHER HIKE.

WHY CAN'T I GO TO A CAMP WHERE THEY LET YOU SIT DOWN ONCE IN A WHILE.

WAYNE

DEAR FATHER,

HERE ARE THE PLACES I WOULD RATHER GO TO NEXT SUMMER INSTEAD OF THIS CAMP.

1. JAIL
2. SCHOOL
3. THE MOON

LOVE,
Renee

DEAR MOM AND DAD,

    THANK YOU FOR SAVING THE MONEY TO SEND ME TO CAMP.

    THIS IS THE BEST CAMP IN THE WHOLE WORLD AND I AM HAVING A GREAT TIME.

    I WISH THAT CAMP WOULD NEVER END. I HOPE YOU WILL LET ME COME TO CAMP AGAIN NEXT SUMMER.

        LOVE,
            RENEE

P.S. ALL THE KIDS IN THE BUNK HAD TO WRITE THIS LETTER.

Dear Grandma,

    I had a very good time at camp this summer.

    A girl in my bunk lost two teeth and another girl had her appendix taken out but I am coming home with everything.

        your granddaughter,
            Beth

DEAR AUNT MOLLY,
THANK YOU VERY MUCH FOR THE NEW BATHING SUIT. I SWIM MUCH BETTER WITH THE NEW BATHING SUIT. IT doesn't keep FALLING OFF WHEN I dive LIKE THE OLD BATHING SUIT.

Best WISHES,
Franklin

DEAR MOM AND DAD,
    I HOPE YOU ARE HAVING A
NICE VACATION AT HOME. WE LEAVE
CAMP ON AUG. 28. YOU WILL BE RID
OF ME FOR TWO MORE WEEKS.
                    LOVE,
                        NANCY

Dear Folks,
            Saturday is the camp
dance with the girl's camp.
The counselor said that
    all the boys have to go to
the camp dance.
            Please write to the
counselor and tell him
that I hate girls and it is
    ok not to go to the dance.
                    Your son,
                    Leonard

Dear Mom and Dad,
    I have a question. Who
do you yell at while I
am at camp?
    Do you yell at my
            picture?

    love, Franky

DEAR FOLKS,

WE MADE A WALLET IN ARTS AND CRAFTS AGAIN THIS SUMMER LIKE LAST YEAR.

PLEASE NEXT SUMMER CAN I GO TO A CAMP WHERE THEY MAKE SOMETHING BESIDES WALLETS IN ARTS AND CRAFTS.

YOUR SON,
BOBBY

DEAR DAD,

CAN YOU SEND MY DOG HUSH PUPPY UP TO CAMP?

WE NEED HIM TO CHASE LOST TENNIS BALLS.

RALPH, YOUR SON

DEAR FOLKS,
    ONE OF THE KIDS PUT
TWO TENNIS BALLS DOWN
THE TOILET BOWL.
    BOY WAS THE COUN-
SELOR MAD. THEY WERE
HIS TENNIS BALLS.
    LOVE,
        Herbert
P.S. I DIDN'T DO IT.

17

Dear Mom and Dad,

I am on the tennis team. The other day in watermelon league I got a bad leg because I was on third base and I came running home and was lying right across the plate and I slid right on the bat.

I was safe but my leg still hurts.

Love,
Tad

Dear Paul,

You were right about camp. They have nothing but counselors and creeps here.

Your friend,
Albert

Dear Grandma,

Please send me lots of candy, peanuts, and cookies quick.

All they give you to eat here is meat, potatoes and vegetables.

Your granddaughter,
Karen

Dear Folks,

Me and the kids in the bunk made up a new song about camp but Jerry, the counselor, said he would wash our mouths with soap if we ever sing it again so I will have to wait until I get home to sing it for you.

It is a real keen song.

love
Stewart

Dear Mother,
    Tomorrow we pack our trunks and leave for home.
    I will pack my trunk as soon as I get the clothes back that the other kids borrowed. If I don't get them back my trunk will be pretty empty.
    love,
    Patricia

HELLO FATHER,
    I DON'T KNOW HOW MUCH YOU PAID BUT THIS CAMP IS NO BARGAIN.

    REGARDS,
    HILTON

Dear Father and Mother,
Could you please ask the landlord if he allows pets in our building.
If he says yes, then ask him what about
Skunks.
your camper,
Jason

DEAR AUNT SARAH,
 HOW ARE YOU? I AM FINE.
PLEASE PASS THIS LETTER TO UNCLE
 JOE, UNCLE MILTON, COUSIN JEFF,
AUNT RHODA.
 I CAN'T SPEND THE WHOLE
SUMMER WRITING TO EVERYBODY.
 LOVE,
 NATALIE

HI JENNIFER,
 WE HAD A MASQUERADE
PARTY AT CAMP LAST NIGHT
AND I WON THE PRIZE FOR
THE MOST BEAUTIFUL COST-
UME. I WAS DRESSED
 AS A HOBO.
 YOUR FRIEND
 SUSAN

DEAR MOM,
   Hello. I took a shower.
That is all that is new.
        Mark

Dear MOM,
        I miss my TV set very
much. I miss channel 4 the most.
                Love,
                Diane

        P.S. Also 2, 7, 9, 11

DEAR BARBARA,
  THE FOOD AT CAMP IS AWFUL.
  THE BUNKS AT CAMP ARE AWFUL.
THE COUNSELORS AT CAMP ARE AWFUL.
  THE SWIMMING AT CAMP IS AWFUL.
EXCEPT FOR THAT IT IS A REAL KEEN PLACE.

                YOUR GIRL FRIEND,
                ELLEN

Dear MOM,
        I LIKE bumble bees
and bumble bees like me.
        I got three bites
                so far.
        ANDY

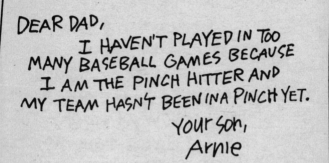

DEAR DAD,
      I HAVEN'T PLAYED IN TOO MANY BASEBALL GAMES BECAUSE I AM THE PINCH HITTER AND MY TEAM HASN'T BEEN IN A PINCH YET.

              Your son,
              Arnie

Dear Grandma,
    This has been my best year at camp.
    I haven't had a cold or a cough and I didn't get any splinters in my fingers
    and I didn't sprain my wrist or cut my leg.
    I have been at camp for two days.

           Kisses,
             Debbie

DEAR MOM,
    Please read the letter I sent to you yesterday.
    We did the same thing again today.

           Jerry

DEAR DAD,

The counselor is teaching me how to play golf.

The first thing he is teaching me is how to be a caddy.

Love,
Albert

DEAR FOLKS,
    THIS CAMP IS THE WORST
PLACE I HAVE EVER BEEN
  TO NEXT TO SCHOOL,
  SUNDAY SCHOOL, AND
    PIANO CLASS.
                Your Son,
                  CLANCY

DEAR JERRY,
    THIS IS SOME PLACE. THEY
GET YOU UP EARLY IN THE
    MORNING. THEY PUT YOU TO
BED EARLY IN THE NIGHT AND
THEY DON'T DO MUCH FOR
            YOU IN BETWEEN.
                Your Friend,
                  HANS

Dear FOLKS,
    Sometimes when it
rains the rain comes in the
bunk, but don't get upset
because all the girls in the
bunk sleep with their rain-
coats on just in case.

                    LOVE, MARY

DEAR MOM AND DAD,
   I DON'T WANT TO GO TO A
GIRLS' CAMP NEXT SUMMER.
   I WANT TO GO TO A BOYS'
CAMP. BOYS HAVE MORE FUN AT
CAMP. GIRLS NEVER DO ANY-
THING BUT TAKE MUSIC AND
      BALLET LESSONS.
            your daughter,
               BRENDA

Dear Grandma and Grandpa,
   Please come up to see
me on VISITING day AUG. 15.
   Please try not to cry when
you see me.
   All the Girls are asking
their Grandparents the
      same thing.
            your Granddaughter
               Hilda

DEAR ROBERT,
        I AM WRITING TO TELL YOU
THAT I CAN'T BE YOUR GIRL FRIEND
  ANYMORE. I FOUND A NEW BOY-
FRIEND AT CAMP.
            HE IS A HOME-RUN HITTER.
NOT A STRIKEOUT KING LIKE YOU.

        YOUR EX-GIRL FRIEND
                AMY

DEAR MOM AND DAD,
    THE KIDS IN MY BUNK ARE
VERY FUNNY AND LIKE TO PLAY
    JOKES. THREE COUNSELORS
        QUIT SO FAR.

            YOUR SON,
                MANNY

DEAR FOLKS,
        Don't send me to this
camp ever again unless it
    is a national emergency.
            your son,
            Rufus

Dear mother,
        I need more under-
wear, socks, shirts, pants
        and hankies.
All the other clothes I
        got plenty.

        your son,
            WALTER

Dear Cousin Ralph,
        NEXT WEEK WE ARE GOING
To have the camp play. I hope
you can come and see me in
    the camp play.
        I have the best part.
    I am the prompter.
            BEST WISHES,
                NAOMI

DEAR JACKY,

WE HAVEN'T GOT SUCH A GOOD BASEBALL TEAM BUT WE HAVEN'T LOST ANY GAMES BECAUSE WHENEVER WE PLAY IT ALWAYS RAINS BEFORE THE THIRD INNING.

WE PRAY FOR RAIN BEFORE EVERY GAME.

MIKE

Dear Mother,
    Guess what happened
at camp today. One of
the boys lost his bathing
suit in the swimming
pool. It was a riot.
        Mickey

Hi FREDDY,
    I AM SENDING YOU BACK
THE RABBITS FOOT YOU SENT ME
FOR BASEBALL.
    I STRUCK OUT THREE
    TIMES TODAY.

    THANK YOU ANYWAY,
        STANLEY

Hello Mother and Father,
  The counselor taught
me how to swim like a fish
but I just want to learn to
swim like the other kids.

       love,
         Richie

Dear Grandma May,

I put a kiss for you on this letter only you can't see it because kisses are invisible.

love,

Diane

Dear Aunt Gloria,

Could you buy me a butterfly net?

I like to catch butterflies but I can't catch them in my hands because I have slippery fingers.

your nephew,

Walter

Dear Sarah,
Monday we had hot dogs.
Tuesday we had hot dogs.
Wednesday we had hot dogs.
Thursday we had hot dogs.
They must get their hot
dogs real cheap.
Sandra

Dear DAD,

HERE IS A PICTURE OF ME IN THE CAMP NEWSPAPER PLAYING BASEBALL.

YOU CAN'T SEE MY FACE SO GOOD. THAT IS ME BEHIND THE PLATE WITH THE CATCHER'S MASK ON.

YOUR SON,
DAVE

DEAR GRANDMA,

We went for a hike in the woods.
We lost a kid.
We found the kid.
The kid was me. That is why I AM WRITING this letter.

Manuel

Dear Dad,

    We need a shortstop, a pitcher, a third baseman and a catcher for our baseball team.

    Please call the Yankees

        Your son.

        Randy

Dear Mother,

    Thank you for writing to me about the hot sticky city streets.

    Whenever I get sad at camp I take out your letter and I get happy that I am not in the hot sticky city streets.

        your lucky son

        Walter

DEAR FOLKS,

I MADE UP A POEM ABOUT CAMP.
ROSES ARE RED
VIOLETS ARE BLUE
CAMP IS OKAY
BUT NOT FOR STEW

YOUR SON,
STEWART

Dear Dad,

I am drinking three
glasses of milk and eating hot
cereal everyday like you said
but I still haven't hit any
homeruns.

Your son,
ERIC

DEAR MOM AND DAD,

IF THIS CAMP IS SO
GREAT HOW COME YOU DON'T GO?

YOUR SON,
ANDY

Dear Folks,
   We are going on an overnight hike in the woods next week.
   Please send right away bandages, iodine and splints.

               love,
                  Scott

DEAR MOM AND DAD,
     PLEASE WRITE AND TELL ME WHAT I SHOULD LIKE ABOUT CAMP.

               YOUR SON,
                  JIMMY

   DEAR DAD,
        THE poor children have all the fun, they don't have to go to camp.

                  Barry

DEAR FOLKS,
    PLEASE MAIL ME MORE
FILM FOR MY CAMERA.
    MY COUNSELOR USED ALL
MY FILM TAKING PICTURES OF
HIS GIRLFRIEND AND I DIDN'T
EVEN WANT ANY PICTURES
    OF HIS GIRL FRIEND.

            Your Son,
            MAURICE

DEAR BILLY,
    I RECEIVED YOUR LETTER.
THE ANSWER TO YOUR QUESTION IS
THEY DON'T HAVE ANY PET ANIMALS
AT THIS CAMP BECAUSE NO
ANIMAL WOULD WANT TO STAY
HERE.
    EVEN PEOPLE AREN'T TOO
CRAZY ABOUT THIS PLACE.
            NICK

Dear Mother,
I love this camp.
I AM HAVING A
WONDERFUL TIME.
Love,
BETSY
P.S. THE LETTER IS WET
BECAUSE SOME OF MY TEARS
GOT ON the PAPER.

DEAR MOTHER,

 BOY, THEY SURE ARE FIXING EVERYTHING UP FOR PARENTS' VISITING DAY. THEY ARE PAINTING THE BUNKS AND MOWING THE LAWN AND FIXING THE BATHROOM.

 YOU OUGHT TO SNEAK UP HERE BEFORE VISITING DAY TO SEE WHAT A MESS THIS PLACE REALLY IS!

 LOVE,
 JANIE

DEAR DAD,

 I AM SENDING BACK TO YOU MY BASEBALL GLOVE.

 CAN YOU SEND ME A NEW ONE?

 THE OLD GLOVE DROPPED TOO MANY FLY BALLS.

 YOUR SON,
 ANDREW

DEAR DAD,
       THERE ARE SIX FIRST
BASEMEN ON THE CAMP BASEBALL
                      TEAM.
       NEXT SUMMER I WANT
TO GO TO CAMP WHERE THERE
ARE LESS FIRST BASEMEN.
              YOUR SON,
              REX

Dear Margie,

I met the cutest boy at the camp dance. I am crazy about him.

He is a third baseman like the boy I was crazy about last week.

Your girlfriend,
Natalie

Dear Folks,

They sure give you plenty to eat at camp. I gained 10 pounds already and I don't even eat breakfast or lunch.

Love,
Ray

HELLO FROM DAVID,
Good-bye FROM
DAVID

DEAR UNCLE MORRIS,
    CAMP POCHAWA IS PRETTY
GOOD BUT THERE IS NOTHING TO
DO AT NIGHT BUT SLEEP.
                WALTER

DEAR MOM,
    I MISS SPOT VERY MUCH.
PLEASE SEND ME HIS PAW
                    PRINT.
        YOUR SON,
            FREDDY

Dear Dad,
    One of the kids broke his leg sliding into home plate but don't worry about me, I don't slide into home plate that way. I slide head first.
        your son,
        John

Dear Grandma,

You are not allowed to send candy up to camp. So if you are going to send any candy to me please put it in a big box and write laundry on the box.

your grandson,
Hector

Dear Mom,

Please don't kiss me hello and good-bye when you come to visit me at camp. I am a real third baseman now.

your friend,
Your son

Dear Dad,
    This camp is a big gyp. I haven't gotten one home run yet.
                    Your Son,
                    Alan

Dear Dad,

This is my last letter. Tomorrow I will call you.

My pen ran out of ink.

love,

Howard

Dear Mother,

I wrote to grandma, grandpa, Aunt Theresa, Uncle Ray, Cousin Hilda, Cousin Thomas, Mr. Pearson and my teacher as you told me to do.

You better send my typewriter. I am getting writer's cramp.

love,

Jonathan

Dear Mom and Dad,
    We have a dance with
the girl's camp on Saturday
and the boys in my bunk
voted 6 to 0 to be wallflowers.

                your son,
                    Ray

Dear Mom AND DAD,
    CAMP STINKS!
  I WILL WRITE MORE ABOUT
        CAMP TOMRROW.

            YOUR SON,
                BRUCE

Hi DAD,
    NO MORE CAMP FOR ME.
  I WANT TO BE WHERE THE
        ACTION IS!
                BUDDY

HI PERRY,

THIS IS SOME PLACE. COOL. SWELL. KEEN. THEY HAVE GREAT RAINY DAY ACTIVITIES. WHEN IT IS SUNNY THEY HAVE TROUBLE.

YOUR FRIEND,
RED

Dear Folks,

Tell Richie not to touch anything in my room while I am at camp.

Tell him not even to breathe in my room.

I miss Richie but not too much.

Kenneth

Dear Father,
I would write you all about camp but I don't want to aggravate you.
Lowell

Hi Robert,
How is your camp. They are very cheap at my camp. They only give you three meals a day.
Your pal,
Rex

Dear Aunt Mary,
This camp is the best camp in the whole world and I know because my counselor told me.
Your niece,
Angela

DEAR DAD,
    You better send my snorkel
    and flippers. I lost my
    braces in the bottom of
                the pool.

        Timmy

DEAR DAD,

PLEASE WRITE ME ALL
THE THINGS YOU WANT TO KNOW
ABOUT CAMP AND I WILL ANSWER
YES OR NO.

I DON'T WANT TO WASTE
TIME AND WRITE THE THINGS
YOU ALREADY KNOW.

LOVE,
BETSY

DEAR GRANDMA,

MOTHER SAID THAT WHEN
I WRITE TO YOU I SHOULDN'T
ASK FOR ANY CANDY, TOYS OR
GAMES SO THIS WILL BE A
SHORT LETTER BECAUSE I
DON'T KNOW WHAT ELSE TO
WRITE.

LOVE FROM ROBERT

Dear Freddy,
   How is your Camp? Don't forget to write. Even if you have nothing to say like me.
                    Your pal,
                    Donald

Dear Mom,
   My Counselor sure is swell. He said if I am a good boy, I could make his bed all next week instead of Ralph.
                    Your Son,
                    Charles

DEAR MOM AND DAD,

THE FOOD IS TERRIBLE. THE ONLY DECENT FOOD THEY SERVE HERE IS THE WATER.

YOUR SON IS STARVING!
MAURICE

DEAR HOWIE,

THIS CAMP ISN'T SO HOT. THERE HASN'T BEEN ONE GOOD FIGHT IN MY TENT SO FAR.

BILLY

DEAR MOTHER,

I HAVE SIX SNEAKERS BUT NO LACES. SEND LACES IN A HURRY.

JAMES

HI NATHAN,
     NOTHING NEW AT MY CAMP
EXCEPT WE HAD THREE FUNERALS
     FOR THREE TURTLES LAST WEEK

          Your Friend,
               Richard

Dear Grandma,
        I am homesick.
Please send me a picture
of your chocolate cake.
                Your granddaughter,
                    Lucy

Dear Mom and Dad,
        We had a big watermelon
in the bunk yesterday.
        All the kids got a big
piece of watermelon but
I got mostly seeds.
                Love,
                    Harriet

Dear Mother,
 They don't have any
holidays at camp.
 You have to make your
bed every day.
 Stella

Dear Mom,
 The best thing about this
camp is going home
 love,
 Sayre

DEAR FOLKS,
 PLEASE SEND ME MY
 CAMP ADDRESS.
 YOUR SON,
 JEFFRY

HI JONATHAN,

THIS IS YOUR FRIEND PETER. I GO TO A SWELL CAMP. OUR COUNSELOR IS SWELL. HIS NAME IS MAURICE. HE TELLS US SCARY GHOST STORIES EVERY NIGHT BEFORE WE GO TO SLEEP.

I HAVE GREAT NIGHTMARES. WRITE ABOUT YOUR COUNSELOR. IS HE SCARY?

YOUR FRIEND,
PETER

DEAR BROTHER JERRY,

HOW ARE YOU? I AM FINE PLEASE SEND ME YOUR PICTURE. I MISS YOUR UGLY FACE.

YOUR BROTHER,
JAY

DEAR DAD,
THANK YOU VERY MUCH FOR
SPENDING ALL THE MONEY TO
SEND ME TO CAMP AND I HOPE
YOU HAVE BETTER LUCK WITH
THE MONEY NEXT SUMMER.
YOUR SON,
RALPH

Dear Dad,
I went fishing today
with my fishing rod and
a can of worms.
I didn't catch any-
thing but more worms.
Your Son,
Arthur

Dear Mother and Father,

We went on an overnight hike and they lost a kid in the woods. Then they found him.

Don't get scared. It wasn't me. I couldn't walk very far anyway because of the large bandage on my leg

your son,
Alvin

DEAR MOTHER AND FATHER,
    DON'T WORRY THE SWIMMING
IS VERY SAFE AT CAMP. EVERY BOY
HAS A BUDDY FOR SWIMMING.
    MY BUDDY IS JEFFRY. HE IS
A GREAT NON-SWIMMER.
            LOVE,
                RALPH

DEAR PAUL,
    WE HAVE 2 RABBITS,
3 HAMSTERS, 5 TURTLES AND
10 BUTTERFLIES AND 4 SNAKES
LIVING IN OUR BUNK.
    I CAN'T WAIT UNTIL MY
MOTHER COMES UP FOR VISIT-
    ING DAY.

            GOOD-BYE NOW,
                EUGENE

DEAR FOLKS,
   DON'T WORRY. I DIDN'T LOSE
ANY UNDERWEAR THIS YEAR.
   I DIDN'T WEAR ANY
      ALL SUMMER.

   LOVE,
      RAMONA

Dear Uncle Jerry,

I am okay. This is the best camp I ever went to in my wole life.

We do all the things I like to do.

I hope the speling is allrite. I asked my counsellor to fix up the speling but he spels wors than me.

love,
Stanley

Dear Mother,

Please don't surpruse me by brunging my brother Eddie to visit me at camp.

I don't like that kind of surpruse.

noel

Dear Mother,
I need a hanky. I have had a running nose for three weeks and it won't stop by itself.
love,
Amy

Dear Father and Mother,
    Could you please go to
the library and find out
about the camp.
    I think the camp was
a prison before it was a camp.
                Barbara

DEAR HERBIE,
    HERE IS A PICTURE I TOOK
OF MY COUNSELOR RICHARD.
    HE IS WORSE-LOOKING
THAN THE PICTURE.
                SINCERELY,
                    HARRY

Dear mom,
   my counselor's name is
Howie. He is 6 ft. tall. He
goes to Harvard. He likes
everything except kids.
         Love,
            DAVID

Dear mother,
   Please throw away
the letter I wrote yesterday
where I said I love camp.
   I hate it.
         Betsy

Dear Mother,
    Don't worry about me. They
have a very smart doctor here
and he says he never saw
    a case like me before.
            love,
                sandy

DEAR MOTHER,
    SOME BOY TRIED TO KISS ME
AT THE DANCE AND I BIT HIM.
    WE HAVE ANOTHER DANCE
NEXT WEEK BUT NOBODY HAS
ASKED ME YET.
            LOVE,
                KAREN

Dear Mom,

We had a good bus trip up to camp and nobody threw up this year except Jerry Pincus again.

He was sitting next to me like last year but the counselor gave me a clean shirt when we got to camp.

Roger

Dear Folks,

Don't bother to write to me any more unless you have very good news like I have been paroled from this place.

love,
Cars

DEAR FOLKS,

THE FOOD AT CAMP IS OKAY IF YOU DON'T LIKE TO EAT.

LLOYD

DEAR DAD,

DO YOU HAVE ANY EXTRA MONEY YOU COULD SPARE? THE COUNSELOR IS BROKE.

SINCERELY YOUR SON,

ARTHUR

DEAR MOM,

You told me IF I WENT TO CAMP I WOULD HAVE A GOOD TIME AND I WOULD LIKE TO KNOW WHEN.

STANLEY

DEAR FOLKS,
GUESS HOW MUCH WEIGHT
I LOST?
MY NICKNAME AT CAMP
IS SKINNY BONES.
LOVE,
ALAN

Dear Mom,
        I would like to ask
you a question.
                Do counselors like kids?
                Your son,
                        Sidney

Dear Dad,
    It rained all day Monday,
Tuesday, Wednesday, Thursday,
            and Friday.
    There isn't much to do when
it rains but if it rains one
more day the counselor
says we can watch him
        Climb the walls.

            Your son,
                Larry

DEAR COUSIN JEFF,

THANK YOU FOR THE LUCKY RABBITS FOOT.
I PUT IT IN MY POCKET EVERY TIME I
PITCH A GAME. I HAVEN'T WON ANY GAMES
YET SO MAYBE YOU COULD SEND ME
ANOTHER LUCKY RABBITS FOOT. THE
FIRST ONE ISN'T TOO LUCKY.

YOUR PAL,

RED

DEAR DENISE,

I CAUGHT A FROG IN
THE LAKE.

I AM TRAINING THE
FROG TO DO TRICKS. UP TO NOW
I HAVEN'T TAUGHT HIM ANYTHING
AND I AM BEGINNING TO THINK
HE IS A PRETTY STUPID FROG.

I MAY HAVE TO THROW
HIM BACK INTO THE LAKE AND START
ALL OVER AGAIN WITH A NEW
FROG WHO HAS SOME BRAINS.

Your Friend,

Angela

Dear Bruce,

I drew this picture of my counselor.

I drew the horns on his head. He doesn't have real horns on his head. We only think he does.

your pal,
Stan

P.S. Please send me a picture of your counselor with horns.

Dear Folks,

I DON'T KNOW WHY I HAVE TO WRITE EVERYDAY. EVERY DAY IS THE SAME EXCEPT FOR THE DAYS THAT ARE DIFFERENT.

SO LONG,
RICHARD

Dear Jenny,

Monday we played baseball
Tuesday we played baseball
Wednesday we played baseball
Thursday we played baseball
Friday we played baseball

I can't understand what a
football player like me is doing
here. Do they need any football
players at your camp? I am
a quarterback and I have my
own football.
                    your friend,
                        Stanley

Dear Grandma,
    I AM NOT GOING TO ASK FOR
ANYTHING IN THIS LETTER SO
    THIS WILL BE A SHORT LETTER.
            Love,
                Naomi

Dear Grandma Herman,
I am having a good time. We went swimming today. Tomorrow we go on a hike. I eat a lot.

love,
Your grandson
Nicky

P.S. Please mail this letter. Back after you read it so I can send it to
Grandpa Louis

Dear Mother,
I took this picture of DAVID.
He is wearing my new baseball hat and I am wearing his new baseball pants.
We are good friends and we like to trade.

Nicky

Dear Folks,
      Here is what I ate
         for lunch.

Monday - nothing
Tuesday - nothing
Wednesday - nothing
Thursday - nothing
Friday - nothing

    I am driving my
counselor crazy.

        your daughter

          Diane

DEAR DAD,
    BASEBALL AT CAMP IS TERRIFIC. I AM THE BEST HITTER ON MY TEAM. I BROKE FIVE BATS ALREADY.
            YOUR SON,
                MORRIS

Dear FOLKS,
        one of the kids in my bunk stole my sneakers.
        Some other kid took my bathing suit. Another kid has my fishing rod.
    I didn't take anything yet.
            LOVE,
                DICKIE

Dear Folks,
You will be very happy to know that I gained 10 lbs. at camp.
I weighted myself yester-day with my football uniform and helmet and spiked shoes.
love,
Jack
WEIGHT

DEAR MOM,

       I TRIED TO REMEMBER ALL THE THINGS YOU TOLD ME TO DO AT CAMP. I BRUSH MY HAIR AND TEETH EVERY DAY. I TAKE A BATH AND WASH MY EARS. I WRITE TO GRANDMA. I SHINE MY SHOES.

       THAT IS ALL I DO. THERE IS NO TIME LEFT FOR ANYTHING ELSE.

          YOUR DAUGHTER,
            MELISSA

DEAR UNCLE JIM,

       THE NAME OF MY CAMP IS CAMP CHIPIWAW. IT IS AN INDIAN NAME, BUT NOBODY KNOWS WHAT THE NAME MEANS EXCEPT THE INDIANS AND THERE ARENT ANY INDIANS AT CAMP CHIPIWAW, JUST LOTS OF PALEFACES.

       From,
        DAVID

Dear Dad,

I joined the boxing team at camp. So far I haven't won any fights but I WILL AS soon as I find a kid to fight that is smaller than me.

Your son,
EUGENE

Dear FOLKS,

We make our BEds every morning. We clean the bunk every day. We pick up the paper in front of the bunk. We cut the grass.

Next Summer I WANT TO BE a COUNSELOR SO I CAN HAVE a VACATION TOO.

LOVE,
RALPH.

Dear Folks,

The food at camp is terrific. All the kids in my bunk are on a special diet. It is called a starvation diet.

love, Paul

Dear FOLKS,

Baseball, Football, Basketball, Swimming and tennis is for the birds.

When are we going to have some real action?

DAVID

DEAR MOM,

WE HAVE FIVE KIDS IN MY BUNK

JIMMY — THE RAT

JEFFRY — THE FINK

BOBBY — THE PUNK

LARRY — THE CROOK

HERBIE — THE SQUEALER

LOVE,
YOUR SON, BARRY
THE FINK (#2)

DEAR GRANDMA,
 COULD YOU TELL THE
GOOD FAIRY TO COME TO
CAMP QUICK.
 MY FRONT TOOTH IS
 COMING OUT.
 LOVE,
 Susie

Dear Mother,

        I met a real cool girl at the dance.

        She is swell. Her name is Susy. She is eleven and she hates counselors like me.

        Love,
        Philip

Dear Greta,

        I won three games of checkers from my girl-friend Stella and I didn't cheat even once

        Love
        Peggy

Dear Mother and Father,

I don't want to go to this camp anymore.

Next Summer I want to go to a camp where there are no girls. only baseball players.

your son,

Teddy

Dear Dad,

Don't ask me how I did in Baseball, Basketball and Football this week because the answer is awful.

Love
Ray

Dear Jennifer,
      I met a real dreamy
boy at the camp dance. We
danced together all night and
I think he is crazy about me.
He stepped on my feet six times
        so long.
          Marsha

Dear Mother,
      Don't expect me to write
anymore. I am in train-
ing for a big game and
I don't want to tire my
       pitching arm.
       your son,
        The Star

HI ALVIN,

HOW IS YOUR CAMP? THIS CAMP IS A-O.K.

EVERY MORNING THE BUGLER WAKES ME UP. WE ALL HEAR THE BUGLER BUT THE COUNSELOR. EVEN AN EARTHQUAKE WOULDN'T WAKE HIM UP IN THE MORNING.

REGARDS,
JASPER

DEAR DAD,

COULD YOU BUY ME BOXING GLOVES? WHEN YOU GO TO THE STORE TO BUY THEM ASK THE MAN IF HE HAS BOXING GLOVES WITH A KNOCKOUT PUNCH.

LOVE,
MICKEY

Dear Grandpa Morris,
   I had a good time at camp.
Nothing much happened
except the toilet was
stuffed all summer.

   So long
      Harriet

Dear Folks,

They are very strict at camp. They make you wash your hands and face every day.

love,

Debbie

Dear Grandma,

The camp is very good to children. I like camp a lot and I don't cry myself to sleep like the other kids in the bunk.

love,

Jenny

DEAR DAD,
   CALL THE FBI. THERE IS A
CROOK AT CAMP.
      HE STOLE MY COMIC BOOKS
                AGAIN.
            LOVE,
            PHILIP

DEAR MOMMY,
   PLEASE DON'T CALL ME
   HONEY ANYMORE.
THEY ALL CALL ME SLUGGER
          AT CAMP.
            LOVE,
            Your Son

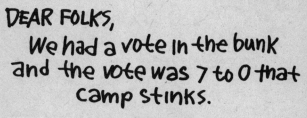

DEAR FOLKS,
   We had a vote in the bunk
and the vote was 7 to 0 that
   camp stinks.
      David

Dear Father,
   I don't think this is the camp that the man showed us in the slides when he came to our house.
   He must have showed pictures of some other camp.
                    Your son,
                        Jimmy

DEAR MOTHER,
   THEY ONLY GIVE US ONE CANDY BAR A DAY.
   THEY ARE TRYING TO STARVE US TO DEATH.
                    LOVE,
                        SANDY

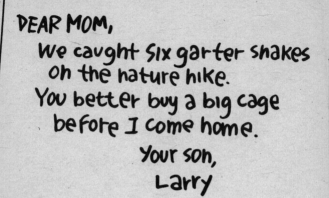

DEAR MOM,

We caught six garter snakes
on the nature hike.
You better buy a big cage
before I come home.

Your son,
Larry

Dear Folks,

    We have a new camp doctor. The old camp doctor left because everyone called him the butcher and he got mad. He couldn't take a joke.

                Your son,
                   Bruce

Dear Mother,

    How are you and father? Is Daddy still working very hard? Does the office still make him very nervous?

                Your daughter,
                   Angela

Dear Grandpa,
 There may be a worse
place then this camp but
 I'll bet they haven't
 found it yet.
          love,
           Your grandson

DEAR MOTHER,
        PLEASE SEND ME
NEW STATIONERY.
         THIS PAPER IS TOO
BIG. I DON'T HAVE THAT MUCH
        TO SAY.
     LOVE,
       GLORIA

DEAR MOTHER,
   WE WILL BE HOME FROM
CAMP TOMORROW AT 3 P.M.
   PLEASE TURN ON MY TV
SO IT WILL BE ON WHEN I WALK
INTO MY ROOM.
            YOUR SON,
            PATRICK

DEAR FOLKS,
   MY COUNSELOR SAYS IF
HE HAD ONE MORE KID LIKE
ME IN THE BUNK HE WOULD GO
INTO SOME OTHER BUSINESS.
            LOVE,
            LAWRENCE

Dear Aunt Hilda,

This is a short letter because I have to go to the bathroom right away.

Betsy

Dear Miss Perkins,

How are you? I am fine. I hope you are having a nice summer vacation. I miss you and all the other teachers but not very much.

Your pupil,
Eric

Dear Mother,

I have a lot of very good friends in my bunk at camp and I am not talking to any of them.

Love,
Lawrence

Dear Mother,
  I am fine.
  Please bring plenty of
bandages when you
come up to camp.
      Donald

DEAR FOLKS,
   I DON'T WANT TO HAVE MY
BIRTHDAY PARTY AT CAMP.
   IF I HAVE TO SHARE MY BIRTH-
DAY CAKE WITH THE GIRLS IN MY
BUNK THERE WILL BE NOTHING
LEFT FOR ME. THE GIRLS IN
   MY BUNK ARE BIG HOGS.

                    SUSIE

Dear Father,
   I think Freddy, my
counselor, likes the nurse
                 very much.
   He goes to the infirmary
every morning and he's
not even sick.
                 your son,
                    Ira

DEAR AUNT ELAINE,

THE THING I LIKE BEST AT CAMP IS WOOD CARVING.

THE COUNSELOR TOLD ME I AM THE BEST WOOD CARVER. IN THE WHOLE CAMP. I GOT FIVE SPLINTERS ALREADY.

SINCERELY,
DONALD

DEAR FOLKS,

I HAVE THE MOST IMPORTANT PART IN THE CAMP PLAY.

I AM THE REMEMBERER. I REMIND ALL THE KIDS WHEN THEY FORGET THEIR LINES.

SEE YOU,
DIANE

Dear Postman:

Do not read this post-card. It is for my mother. You are not supposed to read other peoples' mail.

Sincerely,

Laura

Dear Dad,
    Please send me a
catcher's mitt, a first
baseman's mitt, and a
pitcher's mitt.
    I haven't decided
which I will be yet.
            Your son,
                Nelson

Dear Mom,
    The bus trip to camp
was fun. I like my bunk.
I forgot to flush before
    I left the house.
            Louis

Dear Folks,
    I am having a
wonderful time and I
promised my counselor
I wouldn't try and run
away any more.

        love,
        Carey

DEAR FATHER,
        THE COUNSELORS ARE
GREAT. THE KIDS ARE GREAT. THE
FOOD IS GREAT. THE SWIMMING
    IS GREAT.
            CAMP SURE IS GREAT
AND I DON'T EVEN KNOW WHY
        I HATE IT.
                LOVE,
                MARSHA

DEAR AUNT LOUISE,
        OUR COUNSELOR IS VERY NICE.
SHE TEACHES US GOOD TABLE MANNERS.
    THE FIRST THING YOU LEARN ABOUT
GOOD TABLE MANNERS IS THE
    COUNSELOR GETS SERVED FIRST.
    WE DIDN'T LEARN THE
        SECOND THING YET.

                SINCERELY,
                MITZI

DEAR MOTHER,
REMEMBER HOW I
ALMOST USED TO FAINT AT THE
SIGHT OF BLOOD.
WELL I DON'T ANYMORE.
I WILL TELL YOU WHAT HAPPEN-
ED WHEN I GET A CHANCE.
YOUR DAUGHTER,
Paula

DEAR DAD,
WE HAD A BIG BASEBALL
GAME YESTERDAY.
GUESS WHICH BOY GOT THREE
HOME RUNS IN THE BASEBALL GAME.

LOVE,
RALPH
P.S. I'LL GIVE YOU A HINT. YOU
KNOW HIM AND HE HAS THE
SAME LAST NAME THAT
YOU DO.

HI FATHER,
     YESTERDAY WAS A HOLIDAY
AND THE COUNSELOR DIDN'T
SOCK US ALL DAY.
               BYE,
                 DUANE

DEAR DAD,
          THEY HAVE SWIMMING,
BASEBALL, TENNIS, FOOTBALL,
BASKETBALL AND HOCKEY AT CHIP.
     THEY HAVE EVERYTHING
               BUT FUN.

     YOUR SON,
       ROGER

Mother and Father,
     Send candy, nuts, cake,
bread and cookies quick.
     I can't hold out
          another day.

          Sally is starving